THE WEXFORD CAROLS

The Wexford Carols

ASSEMBLED AND EDITED BY

DIARMAID Ó MUIRITHE

MUSIC TRANSCRIBED
WITH A COMMENTARY BY

SEOIRSE BODLEY

THE DOLMEN PRESS

Set in Baskerville type and printed in the Republic of Ireland
by Leinster Leader Ltd., Naas, for the publishers,
THE DOLMEN PRESS LIMITED
Mountrath, Portlaoise, Ireland.

First Published 1982

British Library Cataloguing in Publication Data
The Wexford carols.
1. Carols, English
I. O'Muirithe, Diarmaid
II. Bodley, Seoirse
783.6'552   M1738

ISBN 0 85105 376 9 *standard edition*
ISBN 0 85105 403 X *special edition*

This edition © 1982. Diarmaid Ó Muirithe
Musical transcription © 1982 Seóirse Bodley

PREFACE

All but two of the carols edited in this book have been published elsewhere in recent years. In 1960 Thomas Wall published Waddinge's carols in a booklet called *The Christmas Songs of Luke Wadding Bishop of Ferns 1683-1688;* and most of Devereux's *New Garland* was published in 1949 by Father R. Ranson in *The Past,* No. 5, a County Wexford historical journal. It implies no disrespect to either of these editors to say that their editions could be improved on. I have edited Waddinge's from the first edition printed in Ghent in 1684, while Dr. Wall used a 1728 London edition which differs considerably from the first. In Father Ranson's case, his treatment of the manuscript sources available to him was superficial; he merely followed a transcript collated by a colleague from two 19th century manuscripts. He claimed to have compared the transcript with other manuscripts, but this is the sum of his *apparatus criticus.* I have reproduced the oldest manuscript copies of Devereux's *New Garland* in this edition and have interfered with them as little as possible.

I only hope that this new edition will have the beneficial effects that Fr. Ranson's edition had in reminding the people of County Wexford of the existence of these songs. Ranson's work helped to ensure the survival of the carols in the parish of Kilmore. A little further encouragement could mean their revival in other places. Oremus.

Diarmaid Ó Muirithe

ACKNOWLEDGMENTS

Our thanks are due to the authorities of the British Library and the Franciscan Library, Killiney, Co. Dublin. We also thank Mr. Jack Devereux and Miss Anna Murphy of Kilmore for the use of their manuscripts. A special word of thanks to Miss Maire Nestor, for her painstaking work in searching for the 'lost' first edition of Waddinge.

for

JACK DEVEREUX

JOHNNY DEVEREUX

JIMMY KEHOE

JACK BUSHER

PADDY BUSHER

LIAM SHIEL

THE CAROL SINGERS OF KILMORE

CONTENTS

9

ABBREVIATIONS

M: Michael Murphy's MS

N: Richard Neil's MS

Oxford: *The Oxford Book of Carols*
ed. Dearmer, Vaughan Williams and Shaw.

Ranson: 'The Kilmore Carols'. Edition in *The Past* No. 5,
1949 by R. Ranson.

INTRODUCTION

Almost 300 years ago, in 1684, Luke Waddinge, in the first year of his office as Roman Catholic Bishop of Ferns, published in Ghent a little book that had a far-reaching influence on the spiritual lives of the people of his diocese, which included the entire county of Wexford in the south-east corner of Ireland.

The book bore the title A SMALE/GARLAND,/OF PIOUS AND/GODLY SONGS/Composed by a devout Man,/For the Solace of his Freinds and/neighbours in their afflictions./ The Sweet and the Sower/The nettle and the flower/The Thorne and the Rose/This Garland Compose.

It contained some religious 'posies', some poems written for the disinherited gentry of County Wexford, and some verses relating to the Popish Plot. It also contained what was to become the foundation of a tradition of carol singing in the county, eleven Christmas songs, two of which are sung to this day in the village of Kilmore.

Bishop Waddinge,[1] a member of one of the principal Anglo-Norman families of County Wexford, was born in Ballycogley Castle, the family's principal seat. The Wexford Waddinges were the parent family of the Waddings of Waterford who numbered among them the famous Franciscan Luke Wadding, the Jesuit theologian Michael Wadding, better known as Miguel Godinez, and Peter Wadding, Chancellor of the University of Prague.

The Wexford Waddinges lost their lands in the Cromwellian confiscation and were banished to the west of Ireland. Luke Waddinge may have been exiled at this time; he speaks in his verses of being banished twice. All we know for certain is that he was educated at Paris, and tradition has it that he obtained a doctorate at the Sorbonne.

Ferns was without a resident bishop between 1651 and 1684. Bishop Nicholas French had left Ireland to seek the

---

1. I have used the bishop's spelling of his own surname throughout. The Waterford branch spelled it without the 'e'.

help of the Duke of Lorraine, but because of the enmity of the Duke of Ormonde he was refused permission to return even after the restoration of Charles II. In 1668 French invited his first cousin Luke Waddinge to return to Wexford to represent him as Vicar General of Ferns. He appointed him parish priest of New Ross.

In 1673 he was appointed Coadjutor to French with right of succession. It seems he was upset at being appointed. He pleaded poverty and claimed that he could not support a servant, but he intimated that he was willing to accept if French insisted. He asked to be sent a pectoral cross, a mitre, a crozier, some vestments and everything else necessary for a pontifical mass, "for nothinge of the Sort can be had here".

Astutely he decided, with French's approval, to defer his consecration as bishop during the latter's lifetime. This saved him from banishment during the persecutions that followed the Titus Oates plot of 1678, when archbishops, vicars general and all regular clergy were ordered to leave Ireland by 20 November. Though Waddinge seems to have been arrested and sentenced to exile, he was able to remain in Wexford by pleading that he was not yet a bishop and had ceased to be vicar general since the death of Bishop French the previous August. In the course of time the hysteria engendered by the plot died down. Waddinge resumed his duties as parish priest in Wexford town where, in 1674, he had built a public mass-house within the walls, a privilege that most certainly would not have been granted without the approval of the old Protestant families of the town, who respected him as a gentleman of the county.

The mass-house cost him £53 and he spent a further £40 on furnishings. He gives details of its glazing, ceiling. thatching, etc. in his account book, and mentions that he had to remove a great heap of dung from the site before he could lay the foundations of his little chapel.

It is evident that he maintained as best he could the dignity of his office and he had a good quantity of chalices, ciboria, pixes, silver cruets, and silver and pewter oil-stocks.

He had a plentiful supply of vestments.[2]

In 1683 he seems to have been asked by the Congregation of Propaganda to explain why he still had not been consecrated bishop of his diocese. He explained that conditions of Wexford town were atrocious: he alone was responsible for ministering to a Catholic population reduced by Cromwell's army from 2,000 to 400. Nevertheless, the Congregation directed him not to delay his consecration any longer and he was finally consecrated bishop in 1683 or early in 1684, the year he published his *Smale Garland* in Ghent. He was an old man by then, and near death.

He left his excellent library in his will to the priests of Ross and Wexford. It contained theological tracts by Gregory the Great, Aquinas, Baronius and Bellarmine, and many books of poetry: Dryden was represented, and so were George Herbert, John Donne and Richard Crashaw. As the reader will notice, the metaphysical poets had an influence on Waddinge: it is impossible not to be reminded of Crashaw's conceit of 'Aeternity shutt in a span' when we read Waddinge's 'Heaven's great treasures are now but small / Immensity no extent at all'. This conceit he develops further in his long carol for Christ's Nativity: 'Now infinite hight is low, and infinite depth is shallow, / The greatest length is short, the greatest largeness narrow.'

Luke Waddinge's carols became very popular, and the *Smale Garland* was reprinted in London in 1728 and 1731 for a James Connor, a Drogheda bookseller.

Waddinge lived only a few years after the publication of his *Garland*. Not long after his death, his chapel fell and his successor was refused permission to rebuild it. For many years afterwards, bishops of Ferns used the Franciscan Convent at Wexford as their procathedral.

The bad days were slow in passing but carol singing was given a new impetus by Father William Devereux, who, on returning from the Irish college in Salamanca because of

2. Waddinge's inventory and will are in the library of the Franciscan Fathers, Killiney, Co. Dublin.

13

ill health in 1728, composed a garland of carols. Fr. Devereux was appointed parish priest of Drinagh, and he had no chapel; the Register of Popish Priests of 1731 gives the information that he said mass in the corner of a field. *(Arch.Hib.IV,116).* Afterwards he built a mud hut to serve as a chapel and the remaining carols in this book, with the exception of the Enniscorthy Carol, were first sung in Co. Wexford in this thatched hut at Killiane. Fr. Devereux incorporated his carols in a manuscript which he called *A New Garland Containing Songs for Christmas.* Manuscript copies of these carols multiplied, and astonishingly they are still being transcribed in Kilmore, a parish that has kept up the singing of the carols in Devereux's *Garland* to the present day. Formerly they were sung in Piercestown, Ballymore, Mayglass, Lady's Island, Tacumshane and Rathangan, but they died out in these parishes due to the neglect of priests who preferred the formality, the chiasmi and the dogmatism of hymnody. The religion of the heart has lost out to what Yeats has called the dead hand of decorum.

Three of Waddinge's carols are incorporated in Devereux's *Garland.* As for the rest, it is impossible to say how many he wrote himself. Certainly he did not write 'Song For Jerusalem', which is English; first printed in 1601, its author is known to us only as F.B.P., a Catholic priest under sentence of death, according to English tradition. I am prepared to believe, as the people of Kilmore do, that Fr. Devereux wrote the rest, as it is clear that they were written by someone very familiar with the liturgy.

These carols are sung during Christmas in Kilmore by a choir of six men, who divide into two groups of three to sing alternate verses. It is no small boast for a parish to say that some of their carols have been handed down from generation to generation for almost 300 years. To hear them sung during Mass can be a very moving experience indeed and those of us who have had the pleasure of being in Kilmore Church at Christmastide can understand the sentiments of the man who was quoted in a letter to *The People,* a Wexford newspaper, in January 1872. 'I have stood', he said, 'within many of the grandest Cathedrals of Europe and under the dome of St. Peter's itself, but in none of them did I ever feel the soul-thrilling rapturous sensation that I did as a boy listening to six aged men on a frosty Christmas morning sing the carols beneath the low straw-thatched chapel of Rathangan.'

They are sung no longer in Rathangan, but the attachment of the people of Kilmore to their very special tradition is as strong as ever. It is with respect and gratitude that this book is dedicated to the six men who sing what are now known as the Kilmore Carols. Long may they live and long may their beautiful songs survive them.

Diarmaid Ó Muirithe

THE TEXTS

PRINTED SOURCES

1. Luke Waddinge's *A Smale Garland of Pious and Godly Songs*

I have reproduced Waddinge's ten Christmas songs as they were printed in the first edition published in 1634 in Ghent. I have preserved the spelling, punctuation and capitalization of the original. I have, however, partially normalized the text simply for the sake of clarity by abandoning the printer's haphazard italicization and following present-day practice in this respect. I have also substituted J for I in the case of proper names and placenames, for example John for Iohn.

2. The Enniscorthy Christmas Carol

This has been published in *Oxford* (No. 14) as 'The Wexford Carol'. I have chosen to reproduce the text of a broadside printed in recent years by the County Wexford Museum in Enniscorthy. A footnote to the broadside, printed by Donegan of Enniscorthy, claims that this text, which is headed 'The Enniscorthy Christmas Carol' was the one sung by a Rev. Patrick Cummins about 1912. Father Cummins got the words and air from his mother, who, in turn, got it from her mother. It is not to be found in the carol books of South Wexford.

THE MANUSCRIPTS

1. Michael Murphy's MS

For the songs known throughout the 18th and 19th centuries as Father Devereux's *Garland*, known nowadays as the Kilmore Carols, I have used a manuscript in the possession of Mr. Jack Devereux of Kilmore Quay, Co. Wexford. On a page he has inserted into this carol book, Mr. Devereux gives the following information: 'This carol book was found in a house in Mill Road, in the townland of Chapel, in a house formerly owned by a schoolteacher named Joseph Colfer who taught school in Kilmore around 1860. The index page was later lost but it bore the date 1803, and was written by a Michael Murphy of Greyrobin, Kilmore, who must have been a local scribe as his name appears on several of the old carol books. This book was given to my father by a local shoemaker named Jack Brown'.

A SMALE GARLAND,

OF PIOUS AND

GODLY SONGS,

Composed by a devout Man,

For the Solace of his Freinds and
neighbours in their afflictions.

The sweet and the sower
The nettle and the flower
The Thorne and the Rose
This Garland Compose.

Printed in GANT. 1684,
28. May. 1685

The title page of Waddinge's *Garland*

The pages of this copybook measure 7" x 6". There are 60 pages but there may have been more as the final carol is incomplete and the manuscript lacks the ornate end-piece found in other old carol books.

The pages of the MS, which are numbered, are stitched together with white thread and are contained within a loose brown canvas cover. The signature of the scribe is to be found on page 40 in the top left hand corner and again on page 46 at the bottom of the page. Pages 47 and 48 are missing.

These missing pages contained part of the 'Song of Jerusalem' and for this reason I have chosen to reproduce the text of this song given in another 19th century manuscript, *Richard Neil's Carol Book*. The Murphy MS contains three songs from Luke Waddinge's *Garland:* A Carol For St. Stephen's Day; A Carol For New Year's Day; and On Christ's Nativity. These I have not reproduced.

Pages 1, 2, 3 and 4 have been badly worn towards the outer edges and many words are missing.

I have the reproduced the MS as closely as possible, using Michael Murphy's spellings, punctuation, capitalization and dialect words. I have interfered very little with this beautifully copied, legible MS My only alterations were (a) to omit a word silently where the scribe has written the word twice (b) where he has obviously mistranscribed a word, I have corrected his error by using the word given in the aforementioned Richard Neil MS (c) I have placed the titles of the songs in capitals, although they were written in the MS in the same hand as the rest. (d) in the case of mistranscribed biblical placenames I have substituted the standard versions for those given in the text.

2. Richard Neil's Carol Book

This legible manuscript is in the possession of Miss Anna Murphy, Kilmore. It contains all the carols in Michael Murphy's MS with the exception of the carol 'On Christ's Nativity', whose first line is 'Tell Shepherds and did your flocks stray'.

I have used this carol book merely to correct faults in the older Murphy MS; all the alterations and additions I have made are recorded in the textual notes.

This copybook, 7" x 6", is stitched to a leather cover and the title page is dated 1819.

CAROLS FROM

LUKE WADDINGE'S

A SMALE GARLAND OF PIOUS AND
GODLY SONGS

1684

SHORT CAROLLS FOR EACH DAY OF CHRISTMASS.
All to the tune of, I doe not Love cause thou art faire

1

FOR CHRISTMASS DAY.

THIS Christmas day you pray me sing
My Caroll, to Our new born King,
A God made man, the Virgins Son,
The word made flesh, can this be don;
5   Of me I pray noe more require
Then this great mysterie to admire.

Whom Heaven of Heavens cannot containe,
As scripture doth declare most plaine,
In a pore stable is born this day
10   Layd in manger wrapt in hay
Of me I pray no more require.
Then this great mysterie to admire.

Heavens great treasures are now but small
Im'ensity no extent at all
15   Eternitie's but one day Old
th' Almighty feeleth the winter cold
Of me I pray no more require
Then this great mysterie to Admire.

FOR ST. STEPHENS DAY

SAINT Stephen had an Angels face
All full of vertue full of grace
By the falce Jews was ston'd to death
For Jesus Christ and for his faith
5   But for those stones in heaven he found
Of precious pearls A glorious Crown.

The Jews doe falcely him Accuse
And in their Councell him Abuse.
Their furious rage without delay
10   Make stones their Armes him to destroy
But for those stones in heaven he found
Of precious pearls A glorious Crown,

The most sweet saint with his last breath
Doth pray for those who seeke his Death
15   And leave not off whilst life doth last
As thick as haile their stones to cast
But for those stones in Heaven he found
Of precious pearls A glorious Crown.

FOR ST. JOHN'S DAY

SAINT John did leane on Jesus breast
Jesus lou'd John more then the rest
Our loveing Jesus St. John did love
His gospell doth it clearly prove
5   Then let St. John be lou'd by us
Who was belou'd by our Jesus.

Divine misteries lock'd under seale,
To St. John Jesus did reveale;
His secrets did to him impart
10   Made him the treasurer of his heart
Then let St. John be loud by us
Who was belou'd by our Jesus.

He was Disciple Euangelist
Apostle, Prophet what he list
15   To him as his most Darling freind
Jesus his mother did com'end
Then let St. John be lou'd by us,
Who was belou'd by our Jesus.

4
FOR INNOCENTS DAY

THE Angell said to Joseph mild
Fly with the Mother and the Child
Out of this Land to Aegipt goe
The heavenly Babe will have it soe.
5   For that his hower is not yet Come,
To dy for mans Redemption.

Proud Herod he doth froth and frowne
Feareth to loose Kingdome and Crown
Full of disdane and full of scorn
10   He must destroy this younge King borne
But stay, his hower is not yet come
To dy for mans redemption.

Herod foreb'are this cruell flood
Of the most pure Innocent blood
15   To thee A Crown this Child doth bring
To make thee happier then a King
From highest heavens along he's come
To dy for man's Redemption.

FOR NEW YEARS DAY

SWEET Jesus was the Sacred name.
Of the sweet Babe who to us came
Angells and men this Name Adore
Both now and then and ever more
5   A saveing name this saviour he
Doth save us for Eternity.

Good God how precious is this Name
He gave his blood to gaine the same
To honour it All knees bow downe
10   In heaven and Earth and under ground
And every tongue confess that he
Doth save us for Eternitie.

Then Jesus I adore thy name
And Ever shall Adore the same
15   Thy name be graven in my heart
Live Alwayes there and ne're depart
My prayers day and night shall be
Save us Jesus, Jesus save me.

6
FOR TWELFTH DAY

BEHOULD three Kings come from the East
Ledd by a star of stars the best
Which brought them where they did espy
The King of Kings and saviour ly
5   With gould and myrh and frankencense
They doe Adore this new born Prince.

It's strange what did these three Kings see
That might by them Adored be
A tender Babe layd on the ground
10   Yet they submit scepter and Crown.
Their gould their Myrh, their Frankencense
For to Adore this new born Prince.

Then let us with those three Kings bring
Our guifts unto this new born King
15   Our Sense our will our wit our heart
And all that e're we can impart
Our gould, our Myrh, our frankencense
For to Adore this new born Prince.

FIRST ON CHRIST'S NATIVITIE

To the tune of Neen Major Neale etc.

AN Angel this night
Doth to the shepheards bring
Most rare and joyfull news,
To move all harts to sing:
5   A saviour from heaven
Unto the world is come.
And God is now made man
For mans redemption.

The Shepheards in hast
10   Unto the stable run,
To see this precious Child
Th' eternall Father's Son;
Without a Father born,
His mother a pure Maid,
15   By whom this heavenly babe
Is in a manger laid.

Now let us, with the shepheards,
Unto the stable goe,
Those miracles and wonders
20   For to adore and know:
With humble wit and will,
And open Eyes of faith,
We shall believe and see,
All that the angel saith.

25   But wits of men and Angels,
Cannot conceive this bliss,
No heart can full resent it,
No tongue tell what it is;

Wits must Admire and marvel,
30   And hearts astonish'd be,
And tongues, with joy be silent
In this great mysterie.

Here's all the hopes of Earth
And the delights of heaven,
35   The joy of all the Angels,
And the great price of men
The ransome of all sinners,
All captives to set free;
How can we but rejoyce,
40   And all must merry be.

How can we but rejoyce
To heare what now is done!
The Son of God made man
And man made God's true Son;
45   God doth appeare on Earth
For to Raise earth to heaven
For what cause of greater Joy
Could ever happen men.

Now infinite hight is low
50   And infinite depth is shallow,
The greatest length is short
The greatest largeness narrow,
Eternity by time
Is measur'd and clos'd up
55   Immensity confin'd
And in a stable shut.

The increated person
Is now created man,
The Creator made creature
60   Who shall these secrets scan
Who made all things of nothing
A nothing is become,

Our God most high and great
Is a poore Virgin's son.

65 His greatness is made humble
And all his might is weak,
His glory is obscured,
His wisedom doth not speak;
His pleasures doe suffer,
70 His treasures Are in want
He made and rules the world,
And yet he's bare and scant.

But 't is to strengthen us
His might is made soe weak,
75 Is for our faults and folly
His wisedom doth not speak,
For to correct our pride
In humble sort he lies,
And for to make us rich
80 Most poore he lives and dies.

The Angels may admire
How these strange things can be
And all the Devils may tremble
Their terror for to see
85 But sinners all on earth
May wel rejoyce and sing,
To thanke, and praise, and glory
Their saviour and their King.

Then glory unto the Father,
90 Who order'd all things thus,
Glory unto the Son,
Who gave himself to us
Glory to the Holy Ghost,
Who did this worke of heaven,
95 Glory unto them now,
And ever more, Amen.

ON ST. STEPHENS DAY
To the same tune, Neen Major Neal

THIS is St. Stephen's day
His feast we solemnize
From him we learn to pardon
And love our enemies
5   He's the first Christian Martyr
Who pass'd from earth to heaven
By suffering hate and envy
And Injuries of men.

More Just than the Just abel
10   This Prince of martyrs dy'd
His blood not for revenge
But for God's pardon cry'd,
For fury and for rage
He did remission crave
15   For mallice he had mercy
And Love for hate he gave.

This souldier of the Cross,
Arm'd not with Iron but faith
Doth not Assault but suffer
20   All that men doe or saith
On bended knees with hands
And eyes fix'd on the skies
With humble heart he prayes
For murthering enemies.

25   He clos'd not up his lips
Whilst he enjoy'd his breath
To gaine for them a pardon
Who did procure his death

Pardon good God thin rage
30   This holy saint doth pray
Lay not unto their Charge
What e're they doe or say.

This Champion of the Cross
To conquer death doth dy
35   Suffrings are his triumphs
Death is his victory
The stones like showers of haile.
Which Jews on him doe cast
Become pure Crownes of Pearles
40   And Palms which ever last.

He saw the heavens all open
His throne of glory drest
His saviour Christ prepared
To place his soul in rest
45   Then let us daily pray
For those who us offend
That with Saint Stephen we may
Enjoy a blessed End.

ON THE CIRCUMSISION
NEW YEARS DAY
To the same tune of Neen Major Neale

THIS first day of the year
Jesus to us doth give
His pure and precious blood
That we in him may live
5   A most rare new-years gift
A greater none can have
A gift more rich and precious
None can desire or Crave.

This gift brings us great Joy,
10   And makes us all admire,
It proves His love for us
To be all flames and fire
And for our sake this day
Jesus is His sweet name,
15   A name which cost him deare
His bloods' spilt for the same.

This name doth cost him deare
By Circumsision knife
For it this day he bleeds
20   And after gives his life
Coverd with costly Red
In his own blood He lies
Prepared to give the rest
When on the Cross he dyes.

25   Both heaven and earth admire.
And doe adore Jesus
To Himself this day severe,
And mercyfull to us

As soon as he's made man
30 And being but eight dayes Old
For us he gives his blood
More precious than all gold.

But how can Circumsision
With Jesus's name a gree
35 The true marke of a sinner
To saviour Joyned be
If circumsis'd how saviour
If saviour why circumsis'd
Why should this marke of sinners
40 To saviour be apply'd.

What's done on this great day
By circumsis'd Jesus,
Is comfort and delight
Wonder and Joy to us
45 Who never had beginning
He by whom all begun
Begins this day the worke
Of our Salvation

Bless'd be this new years day
50 Bless'd be this name Jesus
Bless'd be this day of grace
And mercy unto us
Let's all put on new hearts
To give to our Jesus
55 No other new years gift
Doth he require from us.

ON CHRISTMAS DAY
THE YEARE 1678.

WHEN THE CLERGIE WERE BANISH'D IN THE TIME
OF THE PLOT.

To the tune of bonny-brooe.

THIS is our Christmass day
The day of Christs birth
Yet we are far from Joy
And far from Christmass mirth
5   On Christmass to have no masse
Is our great discontent
That with out mass this day should pass
Doth cause us to lament.

The name of Christmass
10   Must chang'd and altered be
For since we have noe Masse
No Christmasse have we
It's therefore we do mourne
With grief our hearts Are prest
15   With tears our Eyes doe Run
Our minds and thoughts want rest

As Jeremie sadly sate
With teares for to lament
The temple desolate
20   Her gould and glory spent
Soe we doe greive and mourne.
To see no Priest at masse
No light on Alters burn
This day of Christmasse.

25 No masse heard this great day
No mattins sung last night
No bells to call to pray
No lamps, no taper light
No chalice, no rich robes
30 No Church no Chapple drest
No Vestments precious Coapes
No holy water blest.

King David in his dayes
Before the Arke did dance
35 With musick and with praise.
Its honour to Advance
But we our sad Eyes fix
To see layd on the ground
Our Arke our Crucifix
40 Our tabernacle downe.

Our Pictures daily open
As bookes before our Eyes
To read what we hear spoaken
Of Sacred misteries
45 They now are laid asside
And cast out of their place
Themselves from us they hide
In darkness and disgrace.

But if Church wales could speak
50 And Old times to us tell
If dead those graves could breake
Where thousand years they dwell
If that they could Arise
To preach what practis'd was
55 We should have Preists alwayes
Our Aulters and our Masse.

Most pure and precious things
Were given in these times
By Emperours, Queens, and Kings
60 With gould and silver shrines
They deem'd nothing too rich
That through their hands could pass
To beautify the Church
And to set forth the Masse.

65 What those first Christians left us
Written by their pen
What learned fathers taught us
Great saints and holy men
What in their times was done
70 And practis'd in each place
As Cleare as shines the sun
Doth show they still had Masse.

But good Old times are past
And new bad times Are come
75 And worser times make hast
And hasten to us soone
Therfore in frights and feares
Those holy-dayes we pass
In sorrow and in teares
80 We spend our Christmass.

Some news each poste doth bring
Of Jesuites and their plots
A gainst our sacred King
Discovered first by Oates
85 Such plotters we may Curss
With bell and booke at masse
By them the time is worse
Then 'ere we felt it was.

God bless our King and Queene
90   Long may they live in peace
Long may their dayes be seen
Long may their Joyes increase
And those who doe not pray
That Charles in peace may raigne
95   I wish they never may
See Priest nor Masse againe.

11

ANOTHER SHORT CAROLL FOR CHRISTMAS DAY.

ON Christmass night all Christians sing
To heare what news the Angels bring
News of great Joy cause of great mirth
News of our mercifull King his birth
5 The King of Kings of Earth and heaven
The King of Angels and of men
Angels and men with Joy may sing
To see their new born King.

Angels with Joy sing in the Ayre
10 To him who can their ruins repaire
And prissoners in the Limbs rejoyce
To hear the Ecchos of their voice
And how on Earth can man be sad
The Redeemer is come to make them glad.
15 From sin and hell to set them free
And buy their Liberty.

Then sin depart behould here's grace
And death here's life come in they place
Hell now thou mayst they terror see
20 Thy power great must Conquer'd be
And for thy darkness we have light
Which makes the Angels sing this night
Glory to God and peace to men
For ever more Amen.

WILLIAM DEVEREUX'S

A NEW GARLAND

CONTAINING SONGS FOR CHRISTMAS

(1728)

CAROLS FROM

MICHAEL MURPHY'S MS

(1803)

AND

RICHARD NEIL'S MS

(1819)

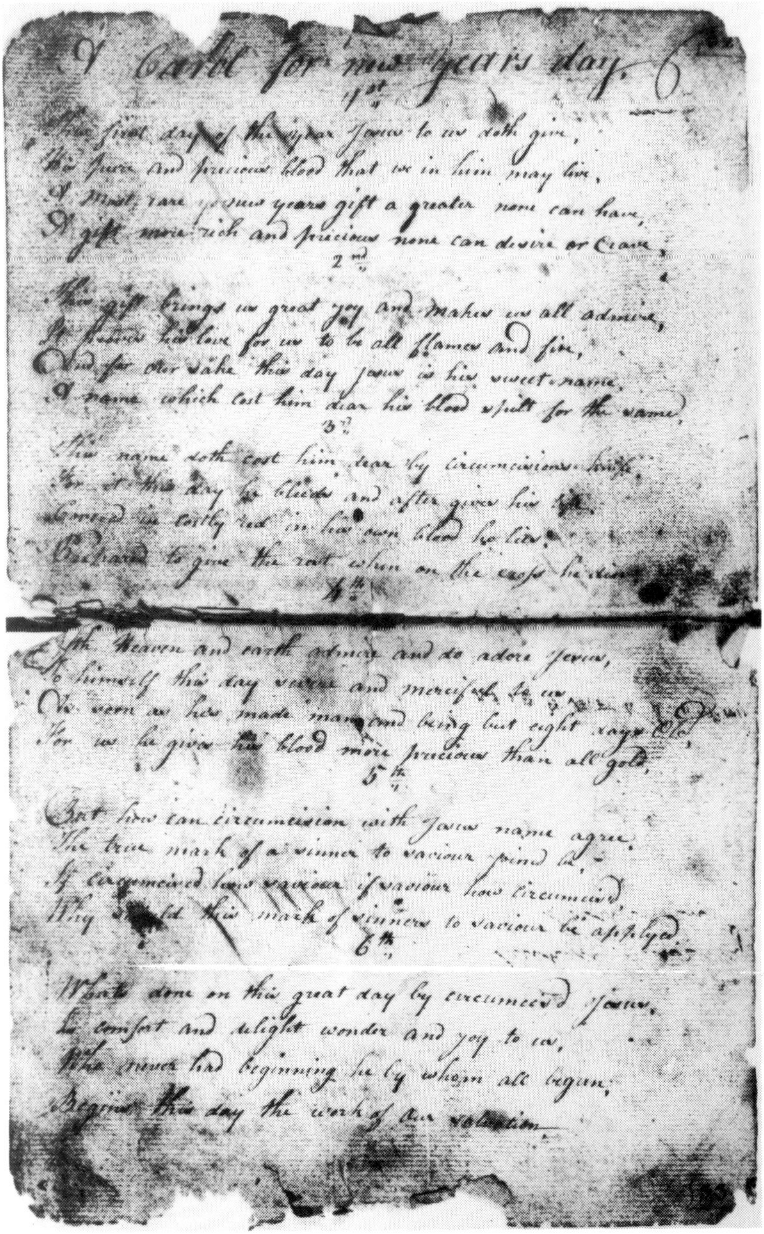

A Carol for new years day. 6

1st

The first day of the year Jesus to us doth give,
His pure and precious blood that we in him may live,
A most rare new years gift a greater none can have,
A gift more rich and precious none can desire or crave.

2nd

This gift brings us great joy and makes us all admire,
It shews his love for us to be all flames and fire,
And for our sake this day Jesus is his sweet name,
A name which cost him dear his blood spilt for the same.

3rd

This name doth cost him dear by circumcisions knife,
For on this day he bleeds and after gives his life,
Covered in costly red in his own blood he lies,
Prepared to give the rest when on the cross he dies.

4th

[illegible] Heaven and earth admire and do adore Jesus,
He himself this day severe and merciful to us
Who even as he's made man and being but eight days old,
For us he gives his blood more precious than all gold.

5th

But how can circumcision with Jesus name agree,
The true mark of a sinner to saviour joined be,
If circumcised how saviour if saviour how circumcised,
Why should this mark of sinners to saviour be applyed.

6th

What's done on this great day by circumcised Jesus,
Is comfort and delight wonder and joy to us,
Who never had beginning he by whom all begun,
Begins this day the work of our salvation.

A Carol for New Year's Day from Michael Murphy's MS.

ON CHRIST'S NATIVITY

1st

The darkest midnight in December,
Snow nor hail nor Winter's storm,
Shall not hinder us for to remember,
The babe that on this night was born.
5   With shepherds we are come to see,
This lovely Infants glorious charms,
Born of a maid as Prophets said,
The god of love in Mary's arms.

2nd

No costly gifts can we present him,
10   No gold nor myrrh, nor odours sweet,
But if with hearts we can content him,
We humbly lay them at his feet,
It was but pure love that from above,
Brought him to save us from all harm,
15   Then let us sing and welcome him,
The god of love in Mary's arms.

3rd

Four thousand years from the Creation,
The world lay groaning under sin,
None could ever expect salvation,
20   No one could ever enter Heaven,
Adam's fall had damed us all,
To hell to endless pains forlorn,
T'was so decreed we had neer been freed,
Had not this heavenly babe been born.

4th

25   But here the best of hearts will grumble,
The faithless Jews will not adore,
A god so poor so mean so humble,
A child they scorn to kneel before,

But o give ear and you shall hear,
30 How all those wonders came to pass,
Why Christ was born to suffer scorn,
And lodg'd between an Ox and ass.

5th
Have you not heard of the sacred story,
How man was made those seats to fill,
35 Which the fallen angels lost in glory,
By their presumption pride and will.
They thought us mean for to obtain
Such glorious seats and crowns in heaven
So thro a cheat got Eve to eat
40 The fruit to be revenged on man.

6th
Thus we were lost our god offended,
The Divils triumphing in our shame,
What recompence could be pretended,
No man could e'er wipe off the stain,
45 Till god alone from his high Throne,
Becomeing Man did us restore,
Let us rejoice in tuneful voice,
Let satan tremble and adore.

7th
If by a Woman we were wounded,
50 Another Woman bringes the cure,
If by a fruit we were confounded,
A tree our safety would procure.
They laughed at man but if they can,
Let satan with his hellish swarms,
55 Refuse to kneel and honour yield,
To the lovely Babe in Mary's arms.

8th
We like beasts lay in a stable,
Senseless blind and dead by sin,
To help ourselves we were not able,
60 But he brings grace and life again.

He conquered Hell confin'd the Devil,
To free your souls from Endless harms.
He's life he gave and now you have,
The god of love in Mary's Arms.

9th

65 Ye faithfull hearts be not offended,
To own your god tho seeming mean,
By this from Hell you were defended
Your joys were purchased by this pain,
The lord of all comes to a stall,
70 And to attend him sends for Kings,
Who by a star are call'd from far,
To see and hear those joyfull things.

10th

O! God altho man did offend thee,
Here is a man that must thee please,
80 Though to compassion none could bind thee,
Thy Anger now must surely cease,
And when our crimes in aftertimes,
May thee to anger justly move,
Pray grant us peace seeing thy face,
85 Of this thy son and God above.

11th

Ye blessed angels join your voices,
Let your guilded wings beat fluttering oer,
Whilst every soul set free rejoices,
And every Devil must adore;
90 We'll sing and pray he always may,
Our Church and Clergymen Defend,
God Grant us peace in all our days
A merry Christmass and a happy end.

FINIS.

13

A CAROL FOR CHRISTMAS DAY

1st

1 Christmas day is come let us all prepare for mirth,
Which fills the Heaven and earth at his amazing birth,
Thro' both the joyous Angels in strife and hurry fly,
With glories and Hosanna's, holy, holy, they cry.
5 In heaven the church triumphant adores with all her choirs,
The Militant on Earth with humble faith admires.

2nd

But how can we rejoice should we not rather mourn,
To see the hope of Nations thus in a stable born,
10 Where is his crown and scepter, where is his throne sublime,
Where is his train and majesty that should the stars outshine,
Is there no sumptuous Palace nor no Inn at all,
To lodge his heavenly Mother but in a filthy stall,

3rd

Why does he thus demean or thus himself disguise,
Perhaps he would conceal himself from cruel Enemies,
15 He trusts but two dumb beasts a feeding on their hay,
He steals to us at midnight that none should him betray,
And his supposed father a Carpenter must be,
That none should yet discover the sacred Mystery.

4th

Yet he does not intend to shun his fate decreed,
20 His death must be the ransom by which mankind is freed,
With a long course of suffering for thirty years and three,
Which must be all complated upon Mount-Calvary.
For those he now reserves himself contented to begin,
In Poverty and misery to pay for all our sin,

5th

25 Cease ye blessed angels such clamerous joys to make,
Tho Midnight silent favours the Shepherds are awake,
And you O! glorious star that with new splendour brings,
From the remotest parts the learned Eastern Kings,
Turn some way else your lustre your rays elsewhere display,
30 Herod will slay the babe and christ must straight away.

6th

Alas to teeming nature we offer rules in vain,
When big of such a Prodigy it can't itself contain,
The rocks were split asunder to grieve our saviours death,
And at his resurrection the dead sprung from the Earth,
35 Can we now expect that on his joyful birth,
The creatures should conceal their triumph and their mirth.

7th

Then let our joys abound now all his grief is O'er,
His victory we celebrate his suffering we deplore,
This was the toil and slavery that getting was for us,
40 Your welcome trice welcome divine savior jesus,
Your Christmass is in glory your torments are all past,
What e'er betide us now grant us the same at last,

8th

If you would rejoice let us conceal the old score,
And purposing amendment resolv'd to sin no more,
45 Then mirth can neer content without a concience clear,
You shall not find true pleasure in all the usual cheer,
In Dancing, sporting, revelling, with masquerade and Drum,
Then let our Christmas merry be as Christians doth become.

14
ON CHRISTS NATIVITY

1st
1　Tell shepherds and did your flock stray,
　Or where have you been this long night,
　Strange visions woke me before day,
　I thought it unusually bright;
5　Especially over yon stall,
　Where my Ox and my Ass I do keep,
　I hastened to see for my all,
　I'ts dawn go and look for your sheep;

2nd
　Be still yourself man they replyed,
10　Your cattle is safe at their hay.
　Our charge at Tour-Ader hard by
　This morn tho in winter is like May.
　And since you seem thus far concern'd,
　Come hither we'll further disclose,
15　The wonders this night we have learned,
　Which happily broke our repose.

3rd
　No mortals more happy than we,
　Whilst mountains and valeys we range,
　Not Herod nor Caesar could be,
20　Whilst rivers and pastures we change;
　But fear and joy stun'd us last night.
　Our Fore-fathers long wished for guest,
　Oh my heart how it pants since the fright,
　He's now in your manger at rest;

4th
25　Friend shepherd you seem more to mean,
　Than I can as yet comprehend,
　Here's people thronged to give their names,
　Persuant to Caesars intent;

A well looking couple came late,
30 Could find no room left in the Inn,
To my stall they made their retreat,
I could give them no better lodging.

5th

Twas midnight the shepherd went on
We knew by the pointers and Bear,
35 A brightness amazing round shone.
An angel amidst did appear,
Fear not quoth he I bring you glad news,
A saviour in Bethlehem just born;
Messias, Christ, King of the Jews,
40 All Nations shall hear of this Morn.

6th

The truth of all this you will know,
A babe in a manger you'll find,
As soon as to town you shall go,
Ye safely leave your flocks behind;
45 On a sudden we hear and we saw,
A host of sweet musick from heaven,
Glory to god on high they gave,
Peace to well minded sons of Men;

7th

No sooner the vision did cease,
50 And we were well able to crawl,
We hastened to the mentioned place,
And found it all true in your stall;
Your Ox and your Ass in amaze,
To warm soft breathing stand o'er,
55 At the Mother and Infant they gazed,
More glory than we saw before.

8th

Well shepherd with patience I've heard,
And you have said great mighty things,
I am not doubting the truth but afraid,
60 This message was fitted for Kings;

A saviour 'tis true is expected,
The time they say is just at an end,
But how can we be protected,
By this babe against Mighty Men;

9th

65 My friends you know I am not learnd,
for more than I have said do not tease,
But since those we have seen are concern'd,
Spite of all men they'll do as they please.
For us we had better say nothing,
70 We'll bring them sweet milk in our cans.
I am sure you wont grudge them their lodging,
And sometimes we'll fetch them a lamb;

10th

O Winter have done for this season,
Get a spring face and smile in all haste,
75 To favour this babe you have reason,
Ye flowers Thyme mint gladen the Nest.
We'll dress your stall once every week,
With all thats gay fragrant and green,
You'll shew yourself fond I mistake,
80 For soon here great guests will be seen.

11th

The shepherds went back to Pen-Ader,
The other goes back to his stall,
To tell you how they behaved after,
In truth I know nothing at all;
85 The Infant is now King of glory,
Thro' the world most renowned of men,
Ye have oft heard the rest of the story,
I wish you a good Christmass and heaven;

FINIS,

15

A CAROL FOR CHRISTMAS DAY

1st

1 Ye sons of men with me rejoice,
And praise the Heavens with heart and voice,
For joyful tidings you we bring,
Of this Heavenly babe, the new born king.

2nd

5 Who from his mighty throne above,
Came down to magnify his love,
To all such as would him embrace,
And would be born again in grace,

3rd

Thy mystery for to unfold,
10 When the King of Kings he did behold,
The poor unhappy state of man,
He sent his dear beloved Son.

4th

From the brink of hell he set us free,
A greater love could never be,
15 The son of God to be made man,
And man to be made Gods own Son.

5th

An angel sent by heavens command,
To a spotless virgin in the land,
To one of the seed of Davids King,
20 These Joyful tidings for to bring.

6th

He healed this virgin, full of grace,
And told Her that in nine months Space
She should bring forth a Son and he,
The Saviour of mankind should be.

7th

25   When Mary, that most blessed babe,
Heard all the Angels to her said,
She to retirement straight did hye,
The lord to praise and magnify,

8th

She piously with great content,
30   Each day in contemplation spent,
Until at length the time drew near,
To Bethlehem she did repair.

9th

She friendless ranged up and down,
To find a lodging in the town,
35   But o! alas that heavenly guest
No pity found in grief oppressed.

10th

She in pain was forced to hye,
Unto a stable that was nigh,
Where of a Son she delivered was
40   Between an ox and a silly ass.

11th

The spotless mother wife and maid,
No mortal had to lend her aid,
Exposed to want and piercing cold,
The Lord of life you may behold,

12th

45   The night of his Nativity,
The people in the Heavens did see,
Strange wonders which did them surprise,
But none the reason could premise,

13th

The learned men thought it to be,
A sign of Caesars' Prosperity,
But some that notion did controul,
And said that Isaac had foretold,

14th

The coming of this heavenly boy,
Who would their oracles destroy,
Their magic cells and temples tear,
Which afterwards performed were,

15th

As earth with a new son is blessed,
So heaven with a new star is dressed,
The shepherds warned by an angel were
To Bethlehem straight to repair,

16th

The shepherds gladly did obey,
To Bethlehem they take their way,
And as the angel did report,
They found the saviour in that sort,

17th

Within a manger there he lay,
His dress was neither rich nor gay,
In Him you truly there might see,
A patern of humility,

18th

Three eastern kings came forth to see,
This heavenly Babe come from on high,
Directed by a glorious star,
Which they espied from a far,

19th
.Their gifts of gold and precious things
They laid before the king of kings;
75 Their homage paid with humble heart,
And joyfully they did depart.

20th
The rumour spread both far and near,
Of the Birth of Christ, Our Saviour dear.
That which king herod came to know,
80 He strove to work his Overthrow.

21st
An Angel sent down from on high,
Then ordered Joseph for to fly,
To Egypt with mother and child,
And there remain for a while.

22nd
85 But Herod full of wrath and gall,
Commanded that both great and small,
All under two years old should be,
Throughout the land slain Instantly.

23rd
Deep lamentations you might hear
90 By every tender mother dear,
To hear their Infants' sighs and groans,
Their brains dashed out against the stones.

24th
This massacre was carried on,
Thinking to murder Gods own Son,
95 His persecution soon begun,
But his hour was not yet come.

25th

He in the temple did dispute,
And many errors did confute,
He healed the lepres raised the dead,
100   At his command the devils fled.

26th

For all those great and mighty things
Performed by the king of kings,
To bring us to the light of grace,
They threw dirt in our saviours face,

27th

105   Let each good christian great and small
Repair unto the oxes stall,
From those three kings example take,
To this sweet Babe your offering make.

28th

Give him your heart the first of all,
110   Free from all malice, wrath and gall,
And now he's on his throne on high,
He will crown you eternally.

FINIS

16

A CAROL FOR ST. JOHNS DAY

1st

1 To a good old fashion tune I will give you a new song,
In honour of the great Evangelist Saint John,
To whom our saviour dying his Mother did Commend,
And then made him her son who was his dearest friend,

2nd

5 Of John seek ye no parentage nor nobliness of birth,
Since he has got a brother, the King of heaven and Earth,
For tho he was a Fisherman taught to the Nets and Oar,
He's now the son of Mary and who can wish for more.

3rd

But ye that are so curious his father for to know,
10 He is the son of Thunder, as Christ himself doth shew,
He is the towering eagle which serves the mighty Jove,
To spread his heavenly lightning and burn all hearts with love

4th

To Christ we are all brothers in grace its plain and clear,
But John amongst the rest is Benjamin the dear,
15 Not one besides his brother search both earth and heaven,
Was so much belov'd by Jesus, by Angels or by Men,

5th

Why then shall we compare him to any of the rest,
Who was the loved Disciple that lean'd on Jesus's breast,
Where he sucked in such Mysteries as not till then was known
20 To Angels or to Prophets or Man but John alone,

6th

Our Church the spouse of Christ was left to Peter's charge
Tho John had greater merit he was not come to age,
Being as yet but twenty he's fit to be a son,
But a husband to the Church you see he was too young.

7th

25 You have seen the love of Jesus and now here's that of John,
Who still stood by his Master when all the rest were gone
Tho Peter trice deny'd him before the cock did crow,
Saint John loyal and constant unto the cross did go,

8th

The most afflicted mother he lovingly did hand,
30 And whilst our saviour suffered along with her did stand,
When Christ said to the Virgin woman there is thy son,
He saith look to thy Mother unto his dear St. John.

9th

No heart can hear conceive nor any tongue express,
Their tears their grief their fondness their love or their distress,
35 All three were so united in that one dying heart,
Tho' two were forced to live they rather die than part,

10th

In short when all was over I'll not raise your grief,
In this great time of joy solemnity and mirth,
For fifteen years he served her as the most humble slave,
40 Untill with his own hands he laid her in the grave.

11th

When John had thus discharged his chief and only care,
He then begins to travel and preach both far and near,
If all his works and wonders to sing we did pretend,
A day would not suffice us our songs would never end.

12th

45 Inflam'd with Peters glory and Pauls he goes to Rome,
Hoping as well as they to die by Martyrdom,
He entered with great joy into the tub of Oil,
In which the cruel tyrants intended him to boil.

13th

When this nor all the rest of tortures they could invent,
50 Could not molest nor hurt him he doomed to banishment,
Into the Isle of Patmos with grief to end his days,
But he converts the people and lived there long in peace,

14th

To see church well grounded he's left till very old,
But the glad hour at last an Angel him foretold,
55 His blood no hands of tyrants would God permit to stain,
But as he lived a Phoenix he died by Gods sweet flame,

15th

His testament and will and constant Theme before,
Was to love one another he said it o're and o're,
Thus peaceably he died but Earth could not contain,
60 His virgin corpse which Angels triumphing took to Heaven,

16th

And now the lov'd Disciple amidst eternal bliss,
With Jesus and his mother dwells in hapiness,
By Stephen we are taught to pardon by John we are taught to love,
By following their Examples you'll rest with them above.

17

A CAROL FOR HOLY INOCENTS DAY

1st

1 Hail ye flowers of Martyrs hail blosoms of heavenly spring,
Hail first fruits of the victory obtained by Christ our King,
Hail ever blessed babies whom cruel Herod slew
Hoping to murder Jesus he slaughter'd all the crew
5 The Masacre was bloody and Inocent were slain,
But after all he's baffled his wicked hopes are vain

2nd

His rage was thus occasioned he had usurped the Crown,
And tho he was a stranger had sat on Judea's throne,
The seventy weeks just ended foretold at Babylon
10 All prophecies agreed that now the time was come,
When the long wished Messias his people should restore,
And the three Eastern Kings confirmed it more and more,

3rd

Those great Indian Princes who travell'd from a far
Guided in their journey by a new glorious star,
15 Arrived now at Jerusalem from Herod did inquire
For the young King of Jews which set his rage on fire,
We are come for to adore this mighty new born Prince,
We bring him gifts of gold of Myrrh and Frankincence,

4th

Herod straight informed himself of Rabys the best skilled,
20 In Scriptures or in Prophecies so plainly now fulfilled,
Where is the place appointed where is Christ to appear,
They answer'd all in Bethlehem and this encreased his fear,
However he disguised it and bid the monarchs go,
And tell him when returning if they found all things so.

5th

25 They went they found the Infant they paid their homage great,
But were advised from Heaven of Herod's ill intent,
Those Kings passed by in silence and left the tyrant shunn'd,
Who vowed to kill the Infants of all the neighbouring land,
In dread to lose his Kingdom if any should escape,
30 After a year he spared not one for fear of a mistake.

6th

How silly is poor herod how much he is deceived,
This babe with utmost joy should be by him recived,
He wants no Earthly Kingdoms nor sceptres here below,
Who brings immortal crowns of glory to bestow,
35 He wants but to make happy our souls with heavenly bliss,
Keep all the rest if lawful and only grant him this,

7th

But Christ was now in Egypt there ordered to abide,
Till vengeance reached the tyrant who miserably died,
And ye little Angels ye died for Christ tis true,
40 Go rest in Abraham's bosom untill he dies for you,
Let Israel be redeem'd mankind be taught and then
You'll grace his glorious triumph ascending into Heaven,

8th

Your tragedy was pitious like roses nipt in bud,
Your mothers quite distracted your cradles filled with blood,
45 Your savage executioners thro' pity scarce could wound,
Such harmless little creatures though you no mercy found,
But still your fate was happy for had you lived to see
Christs butchers or betrayers of them perhaps you'd be,

9th

But now for Proto — martyrship with Stephen you may contend,
He fought for his kings honour his honour you defend,
For Christ you shed your blood and he supplyed the will,
St. Stephen performed the both with that difference still,
You will easily agree and pray forget not us,
That along with you we may enjoy our dear Jesus,

FINIS

18

A CAROL FOR ST. SYLVESTERS DAY

1st
This feast of st. sylvester so well deserves a song,
That you may justly wonder it was deferr'd so long,
He was the glorious pope that happily did bring,
Peace into the church by healing Constantine,

2nd
5   Eleven million of stout martyrs the rage of tyrants stood,
And sealed the heavenly testament of Jesus with his blood
Which still increased the faith-full for three hundred years,
Nothing was left for Christians but tortures death and fears,

3rd
Till Constantine the great a Pagan Emperor too,
10   His predecessors steps resolving to pursue,
Was struck by the almighty with a most filthy sore,
That with scabs and leprocy infect his body o'er,

4th
A bath of infants blood by witches was contrived,
This deed of hell ordered hoping to be relieved,
15   And like another Herod the harmless babes would slay,
Had not our st. sylvester cured him a better way.

5th
This Pontiff by command of heaven brought from his cave,
Apeared before the Emperor undaunted and brave,
Relieved his black design their magic art condemned,
20   Told him the only cure was to make God his freind,

6th

The Emperor gladly listen'd and when instructed well,
Baptized by st. sylvester the scabs all from him fell,
Now perfectly cleansed and to his health restored,
Decreed the god of Christians alone should be adored,

7th

25 And that world he ruled in faith might follow him,
In Rome to give a pattern a temple doth begin,
To honour great st. Peter Christ's vicar hereon earth,
Who suffered crucifiction his head turned underneath,

8th

Like unto a Porter he charges with his clieve,
30 And twelve times full of it of rubbish doth receive,
To clear the first foundation of that majestic doam,
To honour the Apostle and expiate old rome,

9th

The face of things thus altered this mighty prince thinks meet
To leave unto the Pope the Emperor's antient seat,
35 And builds Constantinople renown'd for his name,
With other glorious deeds which eternize his fame,

10th

The blood of martyrs ceaseth the Christians leave their crops,
And golden shrines prepared to gather the relics,
Their Churches rise to peace the Idols are pulled down,
40 Sylvester sits secure on Caesar's former throne,

11th

This throne which untill then was most by tyrants filled,
In aught but blood and plunder and man's distruction skilled
Is now the seat of mercy to mankind doth dispense,
The Treasures of the Cross, of faith and better sense,

61

45 See then have we not reason this feast to solemnize,
And st. sylvester's praise to rais above the skies,
O angel of sweet peace and safety unto men,
May we all by thy interest obtain a peace in Heaven,

FINIS

19

SONG FOR JERUSALEM

Jerusalem my happy home
When Shall I Come to thee
When Shall my Sorrows have an end
Thy Joys when Shall I See

5 There is no dark nor foggy mist
Nor gloomy darksome night
For every Saint Shines like the Sun
And god himself gives light
                    Jerusalem,

There is no Rain nor Sleet or Snow
10 Nor filth may there be found
There is no Sorrow nor no Care
All Joys do there abound.
                    Jerusalem.

Thy walls are made of Precious Stones
Thy Streets are paved with gold
15 Thy gates are all of Pearls unheard
Most glorious to Behold.
                    Jerusalem

No pain no Care no Sorrow there
Nor ought But Peace is found
No Tongue Can tell nor heart Can think
20 What Joys do there Abound.
                    Jerusalem

Through the Vast Streets with purity Streams
The flood of life doth flow
And on the Banks of every Side
The wood of life doth grow
          Jerusalem

25   For evermore those trees bear fruit
And evermore they Spring
And evermore the Saints are glad
And evermore they Sing.
          Jerusalem

Here David Stands with harp in hand
30   As master of the Choir
Ten Thousand thousand times he's blest
Who does that musick hear.
          Jerusalem

Saint Ambrose doth Te Deum Sing
Saint Augustine doth Join
35   Old Simeon and good Lazarus
Hath Each their well Known Songs.
          Jerusalem

Magnificat with notes devine
Our Lady Doth Rehearse
The Virgin all in Choirs Join'd
40   Charming Angels with each Verse
          Jerusalem

Fair Magdalen hath dryed her tears
She's Seen no more to weep
Nor wet the Ringlets of her hair
To wipe our Saviours feet
          Jerusalem

45 They all do live in Such delight
So Pleasant and So gay
That a thousand thousand years ago
Seem Like Yesterday.
                    Jerusalem

Heres the Triumphant Church above
50 We are the Militant Below
The Son of god Came down from Heaven
To Join them both You Know
                    Jerusalem

Lord hear our prayers in this house
Let our Cry Come unto thee
55 Let us Poor Banish'd Sons of Eve
Thy face adore and See.
                    Jerusalem

Untill that happy happy day
We'l Join them with this hymn
Haveing for Comfort and Recource
60 This House of god and gate of heaven.
                    Jerusalem

Instead of Pearls and Purest gold
Our Walls are Only Clay
Our Bodies too of the Same Stuff
Must moulder first away.
                    Jerusalem

65 Jerusalem thou Happy Home
Then let me Come to thee
My Sorrows then Shall have an end
Thy Joys then Shall I see.

FINIS

20

A CAROL FOR TWELFTH DAY

1st

Now to conclude our Christmas mirth,
For the news of our redemption,
We end these songs on our saviours birth
With one that deserves attention
5 Three great wonders fell on this day
A star brought Kings where the Infant lay,
Water made wine in Gallilee,
And Christ baptized in Jordan.

2nd

Those Kings must have known what Balaam of old,
10 Said of a star that would rise
In Jacob's land when he foretold,
The comeing of the Messias,
Jaspar, Melchior and Balthasar,
Set out when they saw the new bright star,
15 Leaving their eastern Kingdoms far,
To find the new born Jesus.

3rd

They bent their course to the Jewish Court,
Jerusalem renowned,
Where to find him they did not doubt,
20 But met with a stranger crowned,
They tyrant Herod shocked at The news,
To hear of a new King of the Jews,.
In dread the usurped crown to loose,
Ordered a bloody slaughter,

4th

25 But for amends in this surprise,
Those straying Kings could visit,
The temple made by solomon the Wise,
The world had nothing like it,
There the Ophir gold they could see,
30 There Diamonds rich and Ivory,
Imbroidered silks and tapestry,
From both sides of the Indies.

5th

Yet nothing rich nor rare in art,
Not finding him could please them,
35 The're told of Bethlehem and depart,
No court toys could delay them,
Their guiding star again did appear,
And to that city straight did steer,
Till over the house resting most clear,
40 Thus bid the monarchs welcome.

6th

Amazed to see the cottage poor,
The stall perhaps where he was born,
Leaving their retinue at the door
Though great they entered without scorn,
45 The blessed babe and Mother found,
Laying their crowns and scepters down,
Adored him prostrate on the ground,
And might have spoken as follows,

7th

Thou King of Kings here in disguise,
50 Whom stars obey and Angels serve,
Who Wealth and grandeur you dispise,
You have given us more than we deserve,

Our beds are gold and Ivory,
Our garments rich embroidery,
55 Set with stones and pagantry,
Whilst you lies in a stable,

8th

Here's gold and myrrh and frankincence,
Not for to inrich you we bring,
But to honour thee O! heavenly Prince,
60 As god as man and as King,
Incense to thee as god is due,
The gold shews kingly powers too,
The myrrh keeps corpse long sweet and new
We have heard how you must suffer,

9th

65 And when the grand affair is done,
The world from hell redeemed,
When God have glorified his son,
At length by men esteemed,
Let our poor pagan nations in,
70 And thy happy sheepfold bring,
That free from blindness and free from sin,
They may in truth adore thee,

10th

What else might passed you may conceive,
In this fond conversation,
75 They bid farewell taking their leave,
Homewards to their habitation;
Farewell good christians farewell too,
Many a happy Christmass I wish you,
With a blessed end hence to ensue,
80 Through the merits of sweet Jesus.

FINIS

21

A VIRGIN QUEEN IN BETHLEHEM

1st
A Virgin queen in Bethlehem,
This day brought fourth our saviour,
To our young king, we'll praise and sing,
And victory for ever,

2nd
5   Hail sovereign Prince our souls defence,
O! welcome hevenly stranger,
Is there no Inn nor place for him,
But in a stall or manger,

3rd, A Virgin queen &c &c &c
10   God's own son doth humbly Come,
From Heavenly high treasure,
To Teach proud men the way to heaven,
Its not through pomp or pleasure.

4th, A Virgin queen &c &c &c
Ye Christians who would pitty shew
15   To Christ in mean condition,
To weep for sin which was the thing,
You will hear of his affection,

5th, A Virgin queen &c &c &c
God one and three that great decree,
In Heaven's high councii signed,
Poor man to make of his own shape,
20   For lasting joys designed,

6th, A Virgin queen &c
The son himself for our relief
To pay for our transgression,
A man to be offered so free,
With love beyond Expression,

7th, A Virgin queen &c &c &c
25 Must I adore or kneel before,
A man so mean a creature,
Not I said he I'd rather be,
A rebel, Devil, or traitor,

8th, A Virgin queen &c &c &c
I'll fix a throne where I alone,
30 Like god himself will glitter,
And man to me shall bend his knee,
And own me for his better,

9th, A Virgin queen &c &c &c
Thus vaunting stood that false proud god
To the Angel's all around him,
35 Some were pleased more stood amazed
Till Michael did confound them,

10th, A Virgin queen &c
The Archangel stout cryed out loud,
Who is like our god for ever,
Can we withstand his dread command,
40 Let us adore our saviour,

11th, A Virgin queen &c &c &c
Proud lucifer prevailed so far,
The third part did him follow,
But with one blast they all were cast,
And hell did them down swallow,

A Virgin Queen &c &c &c
12th
45 Here they remain in constant pain,
Yet scorn to honour Jesus,
And to have man of their own clan,
They tempt us and deceive us

13th, A Virgin queen &c &c &c
I grieve to tell how Adam fell,
50 By satan's false persuasion,
And by his fall had damned us all
And left us no salvation,

14th, A Virgin queen &c &c &c
For poor mankind was made so blind,
55 By the devil, the flesh and adam,
They did adore and kneel before,
Dull sticks and stones for satan,

15th, A Virgin &c &c &c
Cursed be his pride who false contrived,
To cheat eve with his story,
But for this day we all might say,
60 Farewell our hopes of glory.

A Virgin queen &c &c &c
16th,
Glory and pride shall never cease,
To him who us redeemed,
The angels fair left in dispair,
And poor mankind relieved,

17th, A Virgin queen &c &c &c
65 No one man would e'er see heaven,
Had not Christ for us suffered,
But all our sins he took on him,
For which he's scoffed and murdered,

18th, A Virgin queen &c &c &c
But why such pain such toil such shame
70   Did God take to redeem us,
Did not his breath make heaven and earth
Could not the same relieve us,

19th, Virgin queen &c &c &c
But man alone could ne'er alone,
Appease his God offended,
75   Being too mean for to obtain
The pardon which he wanted,

A Virgin queen &c &c &c
20th,
Twas mercy alone that moved God's son,
To be made man that saved us,
And satan now to man must bow,
80   Submit and honour Jesus,

21st, A Virgin queen &c &c &c
So as man did fall his justice call'd,
A man should satisfy him,
And by his grace regain a place,
Mock satan and defy him,

22nd, A Virgin queen &c &c &c
85   Then happy we who now may see,
The Divil by man confounded,
And hope we may at the last day
See Christ in Glory Crowned,

23rd, A Virgin queen &c &c &c
When his throne shall shine on clouds sublime
90   With all Heaven's choirs attended,
May we then Stand at his right hand
To see his foes confounded,

A Virgin queen &c &c &c
                24th,
O! God that snake made us to break,
Thy laws and did confound us,
Jesus we see what it cost thee,
We'll sin no more forgive us,

        25th, A Virgin queen &c &c &c
Our church defend and a happy end
Gain for us all sweet Jesus,
Prolong in peace our poet's days,
Those pious songs to teach us.

A Virgin queen &c &c &c

FINIS

THE ENNISCORTHY CHRISTMAS CAROL

Good people all, this Christmas time,
Consider well and bear in mind,
What our good God for us has done,
In sending His beloved Son.
5   With Mary holy we should pray
To God with love this Christmas Day;
In Bethlehem upon that morn
There was a blessed Messiah born.

The night before the happy tide,
10   The noble Virgin and her guide
Were a long time seeking up and down
To find a lodging in the town.
But mark how all things came to pass,
From every door repelled, alas!
15   As long foretold, their refuge all,
Was but an humble ox's stall.

Near Bethlehem did shepherds keep
Their flocks of lambs and feeding sheep
To whom God's angels did appear,
20   Which put the shepherds in great fear.
"Prepare and go" the angels said,
"To Bethlehem, be not afraid
For there you'll find this happy morn,
A princely Babe, sweet Jesus, born."

25 With thankful heart and joyful mind,
The shepherds went the Babe to find.
And as God's angels had foretold,
They did Our Saviour, Christ, behold.
Within a manger He was laid,
30 And by His side the Virgin Maid,
Attending on the Lord of Life
Who came on earth to end all strife.

There were three wise men from afar,
Directed by a glorious star,
35 Came boldly on and made no stay
Until they came where Jesus lay.
And when they came unto that place
And looked with love on Jesus' face,
In faith they humbly knelt to greet
40 With gifts of gold and incense sweet.

Come let us then our tribute pay
To our good God, as well we may,
For all His grace and mercy shown,
Thro' His Son to us, till then unknown.
45 And when thro' life we wend our way,
'Mid trials and sufferings, day by day,
In faith and hope, whate'er befall,
We'll wait in peace His holy call.

TRANSCRIPTIONS OF THE CAROLS SUNG IN KILMORE

Transcriptions and notes by Seóirse Bodley.

Singer : Jack Devereux, *a fisherman, aged 70.*

Recorded in April, 1980, by Diarmaid Ó Muirithe.

NOTES ON THE TRANSCRIPTIONS

In order to distinguish between the ornaments and the basic melody, while at the same time making the music as easy to read as possible, I have adopted the following procedures:

1. The basic melody is written in standard notation, and all ornaments are indicated by signs common in classical music, with additions where necessary. (Though these signs refer to the same *notes* as are used in much classical music for the indicated ornaments, the rhythmic execution is quite different, as explained below).

2. All the melodies are written down in keys commonly used in Irish traditional music. The melodies however cannot all be played in their entirety on all traditional instruments without octave (or other) transposition.. To have placed the melodies in ranges suited to traditional instrumental performance would have resulted in the use of unvocal ranges.

Basically only three types of sign are used:

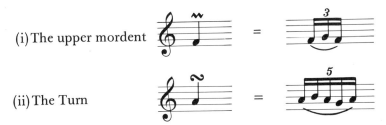

(i) The upper mordent

(ii) The Turn

(iii) Grace notes and other ornaments (indicated by a stroke through the tail)

A straight horizontal line has been added to the basic signs to indicate a held note. This shows either that the ornament comes at the end of the note ⎯⎯⎯ⱳ , or at the beginning of the note ℘⎯⎯⎯

For example:

Where the sign for an upper mordent at the end of a note ⎯⎯⎯ⱳ is applied to a note of a short time-value a pause on the note is intended.

In cases where an ornament is followed by grace-notes there should be no break between them.

THE PERFORMANCES

In general the ornaments and grace-notes were sung at a sufficiently slow pace to make them clear and unhurried in execution. All the mordents and turns followed always *after* the accent, never before:

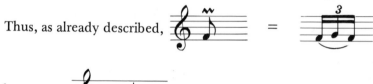

but never

In those cases where ornamental notes came *before* the accent, grace-notes (♪ ♫ etc.) are used.

Many of the melody notes were approached from below. When the note directly below the melody-note was clearly sounded, it is indicated by a grace-note:

When the approach to the melody-note was indefinite in pitch a small diagonal line indicates a short glissando or slide. In different performances of the same melody the singer used the same repertoire of ornaments — but not always on exactly the same notes. The melody itself was fundamentally unaltered.

The overall speed of these carols is very slow indeed. The Carol for Holy Innocents Day, for example, had as its basic tempo ♪ = 72 M.M.

In general the tempo was considerably slower than that used in most ornamented traditional singing in Irish. The speed fluctuated in an Irish *tempo rubato* in keeping with the music, slowing to accommodate ornaments where they demanded extra time. At all times the musical tension was maintained, whether the music slowed or not.

Those wishing to attempt to sing these songs might care to learn the words and basic melody first, omitting all ornaments and grace-notes. Having studied the repertoire of ornaments and where they were used in these performances, a singer could then endeavour to apply the ornaments to the tunes in a suitable manner, without trying to reproduce exactly the original performances.

Seóirse Bodley

Hail — ye flow'rs of — mar- tyrs, hail —
bloss-oms of heav'n - ly spring! Hail
first fruits of — the vic -to - ry — obtained by Christ our — King. Hail
ev - er bless - ed — bab - ies — whom
cru - el Her - od slew Hop -
ing to mur - der Jes - us he

slaugh-tered all the __ crew. The

mas - sa-cre __ was __ bloo - dy, __ the

in - no - cents __ are slain, But af - ter __ all __ he's

baff - led, his wi -cked hopes are vain.

SONG FOR JERUSALEM

Jer - us - al - em __ our hap - py home

When shall __ we come __ to __ thee? When

shall— our sorr - ows have— an— end, Thy

joys — when shall — we see?

A CAROL FOR TWELFTH DAY

Now to con-clude our Christ - mas mirth With the

news of— our re - demp - tion We will

end our— songs on our Sav - iour's birth With —

one that de-serves at - ten - tion.

Three great won - ders fell on this day— A __
star brought kings where the In - fant lay, __
Wat- er made wine in Ga - li- lee, __ And __
Christ bap- tised in __ Jor - dan.

ON CHRIST'S NATIVITY

The dark-est mid - night in De - cem'-ber No
snow nor hail __ nor win - ter storms shall
hin - der us __ for to re - mem-ber The

84

babe that on — this night was born. With —

shep-herds we — are come to — see — This

love - ly In - fants glor-ious charms Born —

of a — maid — as pro - phets said — The

God of — love — in Ma - ry's arms. —

A CAROL FOR CHRISTMAS DAY, the first line of which
is 'Christmas Day is come, let us all prepare for mirth', was
sung by this singer to the music of the CAROL FOR HOLY
INOCENTS' DAY, the first line of which is 'Hail ye flowers
of martyrs'.

of which the first line is 'Ye sons of men with me rejoice'.

Ye — sons of men — with me re-joice And —

praise the heavens with heart and voice — For

joy-ful tid - ings — you we bring Of this

Heav'n - ly Babe— and new - born King. —

THE ENNISCORTHY CHRISTMAS CAROL, 'Good people all', was sung by this singer to the melody of A Carol For Christmas Day — 'Ye sons of men'.

ON ST. STEPHEN'S DAY

This is Saint Steph-en's Day, — his — feast we sol-em — nise; From him we learn to par - don — and love our en - em - ies. He's the first Christ - ian mar - tyr that passed from earth — to — heav'n By suff' - ring hate and — en - vy and in - jur - ies — by men.

A CAROL FOR ST. JOHN'S DAY, A CAROL FOR ST. SYLVESTER'S DAY and the SONG ON THE CIRCUMCISION, NEW YEAR'S DAY, were all sung by this singer to the melody of ON ST. STEPHEN'S DAY.

ORIGINAL KEYS AND TEMPI:— *

Title	Speed	Original Key Signature
A Carol for Holy Innocents Day	♪ = 72 MM	A♭ Major
Song for Jerusalem	♪ = 80 MM	E Major
Carol for Twelfth Day	♪ = 80 MM	G♭ Major
On Christ's Nativity	♪ = 72 MM	A♭ Major
A Carol for Christmas Day (ye Sons of Men)	♪ = 84 MM	D♭ Major
On St. Stephen's Day	♪ = 84 MM	D♭ Major

*All tempi were subject to much *rubato*. The metronome markings are approximate indications of the basic tempo.

NOTES ON THE TEXTS

1 – 6

As far as I know these carols were not included in Fr. Devereux's *Garland*. They are not in M or N nor are they in the repertoire of today's Kilmore carol singers.

7

12 Son;] Ion
14 pure] purc

This carol is no longer sung in Kilmore, although it is to be found in manuscripts transcribed as late as 1944. Stanza 7 is omitted in most manuscripts transcribed after 1940 although it is included in M and in N. Ranson (p. 80) suggests that the Neen Major Neal (Major Neal's Daughter) who gave her name to the air may have been Onor nyn Neal (Honor O'Neal) of Old Ross, who in 1663, July 2nd was pardoned for having broken the peace. (Fiants Eliz. 6660). Formerly sung in Kilmore to the air of 9. Perhaps this air and Neen Major Neal are one and the same.

8.

This carol is still sung in Kilmore.

9

This carol is still sung in Kilmore.

10

This was not included in Fr. Devereux's Garland, and is not found in M or in N. It is not sung in Kilmore.

11

This carol is not sung in Kilmore.

12

Words missing from M and supplied by N:
7 Born 25 grumble, 26 The 28 A 34 How 35 Which 36 By 37 They
38 Such, heaven 56 To 57 We like

This carol is still sung in Kilmore. The first 3 stanzas and stanza 7 were contributed by Grattan Flood, a Wexford musicologist, to R. Dunstan's 'Christmas Carols' Book I, p. 27. Flood sets the carol to the air 'The Foggy Dew' and he wrongly attributes the words to Luke Waddinge.

13

48 Christians N] Christmas M.

Grattan Flood contributed this carol to R. Dunstan's 'Christmas Carols' Book II, p. 30. Flood suggested that it be sung to the air 'The Brown Little Mallet'. Ranson (p. 74) says that the last stanza used to be omitted by the Lady's Island carol singers, 'lest the references in the last lines should be wrongly interpreted'.

14

11 Tour-Ader: cf Tur, Aramaic, 'a mountain'; Eder, Hebrew, 'flock'.
47 they] the M
79 I cannot make sense of this line.
80 For] Or M.
81 Pen: Possibly metathesized from Hebrew Pne, 'towards'

This is the carol referred to by Ranson (p. 71) as the 'lost Carol for Midnight Mass'. It is strange that he did not notice that the fragment he quotes from it was part of 13 in M, a manuscript he claimed to have examined.

15

M ends at 108; last verse is from N.

This carol is not now sung in Kilmore. The leader of the Kilmore carol singers, Mr. Jack Devereux, tells me that it was formerly sung before the priest came on the altar on Christmas Day, and that it was the last sung in Kilmore in 1850 when his grandfather sang in the choir for the first time. We are indebted to the Devereux family for preserving the air to which this carol was sung.

4 dearest friend, N] friend M
11 towering eagle N] towering which M.

This carol is sung in Kilmore

22 Bethlehem] Bethlam M

Sung in Kilmore to the air of 12.

29 a Porter N] Porter M   clieve = Irish *cliabh*, 'a basket'
38 relics, N] relicts M.

Sung in Kilmore.

1   happy] Heavenly N 'happy' in all other Kilmore MSS
27 the Saints] they are N.
33 doth Te Deum sing] doth with Tedeum Sing N.
35 Simeon] Simon N   Lazarus] Laharie N.

Sung in Kilmore at the first Mass on Twelfth Day. Ranson has an intriguing
note: 'Mr. James Howlin of Kilmore, writing to "The People", January 20th
1872, says: "It appears the song was originally written by a Father Bennett,
a Franciscan martyr, while in a prison in Lancashire, in the reign of
Elizabeth." I have been unable to check any authority for Mr. Howlin's
statement.'

The author of 'Jerusalem my Happy home' is known to us only as 'F.B.P.'
In the light of Mr. Howlin's statement, which concurrs with English
tradition, could 'F.B.P.' not stand for F. Bennett, Priest? A version of this
song (which contains many reminiscences and some borrowings from a
slightly older song called 'O Mother dear, Jerusalem' by W. Pridd) is dated
about 1600.

29 Ophir] oppher N.M. cf. Psalm 45, 10.

Sung in Kilmore

21

This carol is no longer sung in Kilmore. The words are to be found in
manuscripts copied as late as 1950 but the air to which it used to be sung is
lost.

22

24 born.] born."

The words of this carol, which is not found in any of the carol books of
south Wexford, and which is not known in Kilmore, may be English.

The carol is in *Oxford* (No. 14), communicated by Grattan Flood. The
Enniscorthy broadside is identical to *Oxford 14* except that it contains an
extra stanza — the last one. The first four and a half verses are in
Shawcross's *Old Castleton Christmas Carols,* a book of Derbyshire songs,
and the first verse was given to R. Vaughan Williams by a Derbyshire man
who sang them to a different air. See *Eight Traditional English Carols,*
No. 7 ed. Vaughan Williams.

BIBLIOGRAPHY

This Bibliography gives details of books cited and of some others which I have used but have not found necessary to cite.

Waddinge, Luke, *A Smale Garland of Pious and Godly Songs.* (Ghent 1684). Other editions, London 1728 and 1731.

Dearmer, P.; Vaughan Williams, R.; Shaw, M. *The Oxford Book of Carols* (London 1928)

Dunstan, R. Christmas Carols Books 1 and 11 (London 1908)

Greene, R.L., *Early English Carols* (London 1935)

Grierson, H., *Poetic Works of John Donne* (Oxford 1966)

Husk, W.H., Songs of the Nativity (London 1868)

Lewis, C.S., *English Literature in the Sixteenth Century Excluding Drama* (Oxford 1954)

Manning, B.L., *The Hymns of Wesley & Watts* (London 1942)

Martin, L.C., *The Poems of Richard Crashaw* (Oxford 1957)

Martin L.C., *Poetic Works of Herrick* (London 1956)

Mayo, C.H., *Traditional Carols* (London 1893)

Phillips, C.S., *Hymnody Past and Present* (London 1937)

Ranson, R. *"The Kilmore Carols"*, The Past, Vol. 5, (Wexford 1949)

Rickert, E., *Ancient English Chistmas Carols* (London 1914)

Rowley, E., *The English Carol* (London 1958)

Shawcross, W.H., *Old Castleton Christmas Carols* (London 1904)

Wall, T. *The Christmas Songs of Luke Waddinge, Bishop of Ferns 1683-1688.* (Dublin 1960)

Williams, R. Vaughan, *Eight Traditional English Carols* (London 1928)

INDEX OF FIRST LINES

This first day of the year
Text p. 32; Air p. 87.

This is our Christmass day
Text p. 34; Air unknown.

This is St Stephen's day
Text p. 30; Air p. 87.

To a good old fashion tune I will give you a new song
Text p. 54; Air p. 87.

Ye sons of men with me rejoice
Text p. 49; Air p. 86.